Let's Explore Science

YOU CAN'T WEAR THESE GENES

SHIRLEY DUKE

ROURKE PUBLISHING

www.rourkepublishing.com

www.rourkepublishing.com

Photo credits: Mark Evans/iStockphoto, cover; Andrey Volodin/iStockphoto, cover, 1; Supri Suharjoto/Shutterstock Images, 4; AP Images, 5; Dorling Kindersley, 6, 9, 10, 13, 14, 16, 18, 26, 30, 35, 39; Ben Greer/iStockphoto, 7; Nicholas Monu/iStockphoto, 8; Jaren Jai Wicklund/Shutterstock Images, 11 (top); Monika Adamczyk/iStockphoto, 11 (middle); Oleg Prikhodko/iStockphoto, 11 (bottom); Eugene Llacuna/iStockphoto, 12; iStockphoto, 15 (left), 17, 19; Erik Lam/iStockphoto, 15 (right); David H. Lewis/iStockphoto, 20; Hulton Archive/Getty Images, 21; Shutterstock Images, 22, 23; Radu Razvan/iStockphoto, 24; Filippova Olga/iStockphoto, 25; Liza McCorkle/iStockphoto, 27; Linda Kloosterhof/iStockphoto, 28; Michael Krinke/iStockphoto, 29; Vladimír Vítek/iStockphoto, 31; Phil Morley/iStockphoto, 32; G W Willis/Photolibrary, 33; David Marchal/iStockphoto, 34, 40; Skip Odonnell/iStockphoto, 36; Paul Sakuma/AP Images, 37; Evan Vucci, File/AP Images, 38; Alexandre Meneghini/AP Images, 41; Red Line Editorial, Inc., 42; Valentin Vitanov/Fotolia, 42 (top); Paul Laroque/Fotolia, 42 (bottom); AP Images, 43; Monkey Business Images/Shutterstock Images, 44; Shutterstock Images, 45

Editor: Holly Saari

Cover and page design: Kazuko Collins

Content Consultant: Richard K. Wilson, PhD, Professor of Genetics and Molecular Microbiology, Washington University, St. Louis, Missouri

Library of Congress Cataloging-in-Publication Data

Duke, Shirley Smith.
  You can't wear these genes / Shirley Duke.
     p. cm. -- (Let's explore science)
  Includes bibliographical references and index.
  ISBN 978-1-61590-324-5 (hard cover)(alk. paper)
  ISBN 978-1-61590-563-8 (soft cover)
  1. Genetics--Juvenile literature. I. Title.
  QH437.5.D85 2011
  576.5--dc22
                           2010009911

Rourke Publishing
Printed in the United States of America, North Mankato, Minnesota
033010
033010LP

www.rourkepublishing.com - rourke@rourkepublishing.com
Post Office Box 643328 Vero Beach, Florida 32964

Table of Contents

Chapter 1

ALL IN THE GENES

"You have your mother's green eyes."

"Your chin comes from your father."

"You must get your musical ability from your parents."

People have always noticed traits, or characteristics, that are similar between parents and their kids. Some of these traits, such as eye color and a dimpled chin, can be easily seen. Other traits, like blood type and personality, cannot be seen.

Scientists who study genetics are called geneticists.

Parents pass down traits to their **offspring**, or young. The offspring have these inherited traits for the rest of their lives. **Genetics** is the branch of science that studies how traits are passed along.

To understand how genetics works, look inside a cell. All living things are made of tiny cells, such as skin cells, nerve cells, and blood cells.

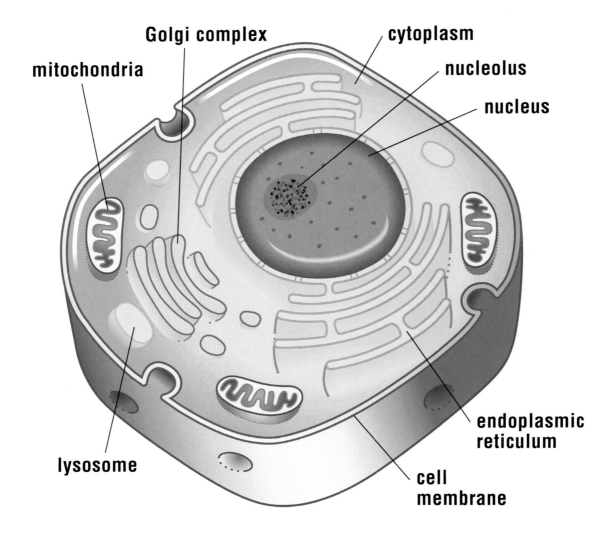

mitochondria

Golgi complex

cytoplasm

nucleolus

nucleus

endoplasmic
reticulum

lysosome

cell
membrane

Each cell has a nucleus, which is the cell's control center. Every nucleus carries all the information a living thing needs to grow, live, and reproduce. This information is tightly packaged in a coil, which looks like a wound-up rope or hose. The coil is made of long, threadlike structures called **chromosomes**.

Deoxyribonucleic acid, or DNA, forms the
chromosomes. DNA is at the very heart of genetics. A
DNA molecule is incredibly complex. It looks like a twisted
ladder. Four bases, or basic building blocks, make up the
"rungs" of the ladder. Bases always come in pairs. Each
rung in the ladder is made of two out of the four bases.

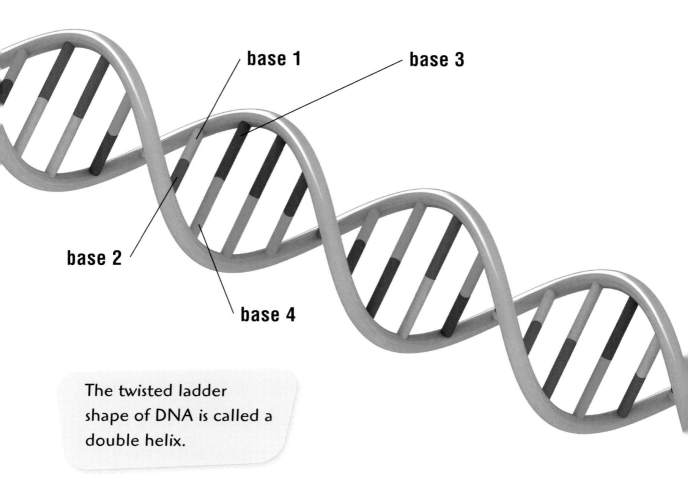

base 1

base 3

base 2

base 4

The twisted ladder
shape of DNA is called a
double helix.

DID YOU KNOW?

Inherited traits cannot explain everything about why living things look and act the way they do. Environment and experience also play a part. Traits that are not inherited are called acquired traits. For example, if an athlete lifts weights a lot, his or her big muscles are an acquired trait.

The order of the rungs and the combination of the bases make up a kind of code. The code carries instructions about how a living thing should grow, change, and operate. DNA is the reason **species** are distinct. Human babies are always born to humans, kittens are born to cats, and sunflowers make more sunflowers.

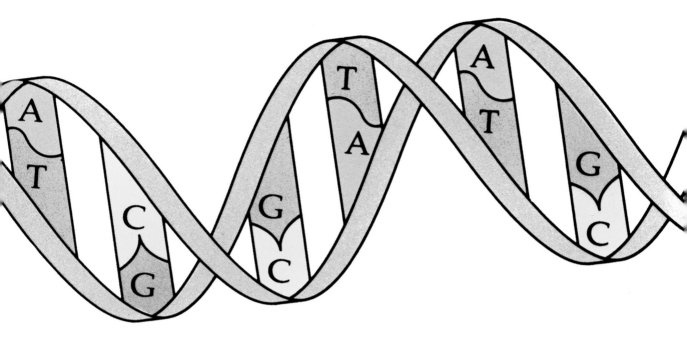

The four DNA bases are adenine, thymine, guanine, and cytosine. Adenine only pairs with thymine. Guanine only pairs with cytosine. Scientists often refer to the bases by their first initials.

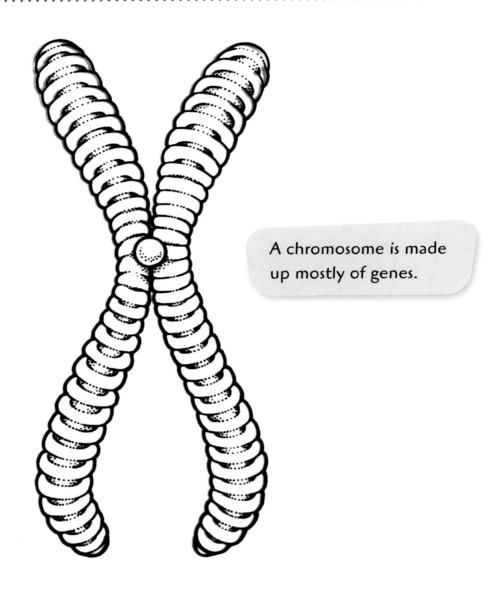

A chromosome is made up mostly of genes.

A **gene** is made up of just a tiny section of a DNA ladder. In humans, a single DNA molecule contains 20,000 to 25,000 genes. Each gene carries just one part of the code. It passes along its instructions through chemical reactions that occur inside the cell.

DID YOU KNOW?

Can you wiggle your ears? If so, you inherited that trait from your parents. Here are some other traits that are passed down through genes:

◉ When you smile, do you get dimples in your cheeks? Chances are, so does someone else in your family. Dimples are inherited.

◉ Look at your toes. Is your second toe longer or shorter than your big toe? The answer to that question depends on your genes.

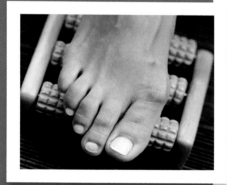

◉ Stick out your thumb. How far back does the top part go? Some people cannot bend it back at all. Others can bend it way back. How much it bends depends on DNA.

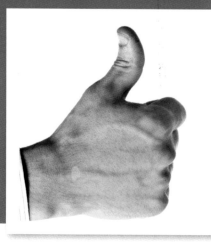

Chapter 2

FROM CELL TO CELL

ells make a person grow and develop. They also do much of the work in the body. Doing that work makes the cells wear out and die. New cells must be made constantly. They need DNA to provide the blueprint, or master plan.

The body continually produces new skin cells to take the place of cells that have died.

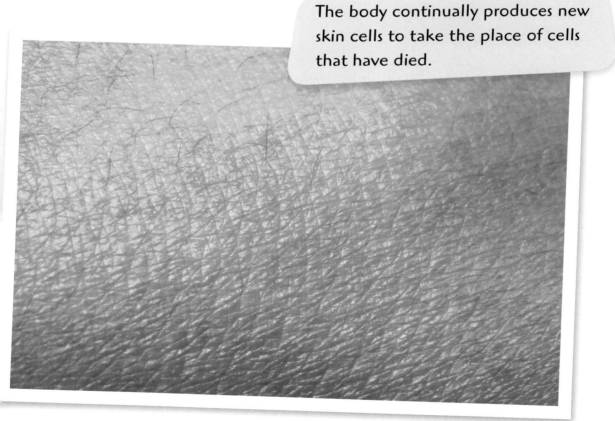

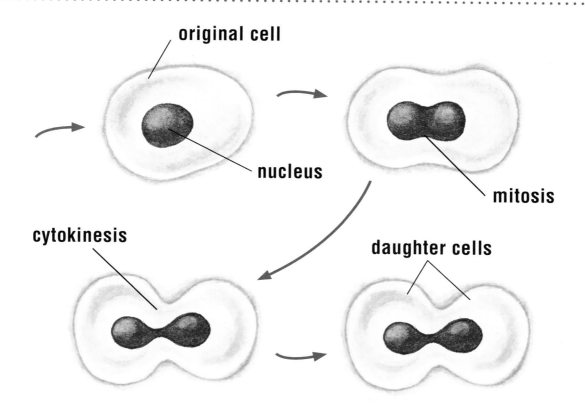

original cell

nucleus

mitosis

cytokinesis

daughter cells

Body cells divide during processes called mitosis and cytokinesis. The nucleus divides during mitosis. The rest of the cell divides during cytokinesis.

A cell makes another cell by dividing in two. Unlike dividing a number in math, a dividing cell does not get smaller. It creates a new cell exactly like itself. Every cell has to keep the same number of chromosomes in its nucleus. In humans, each cell has 46 chromosomes arranged in 23 pairs.

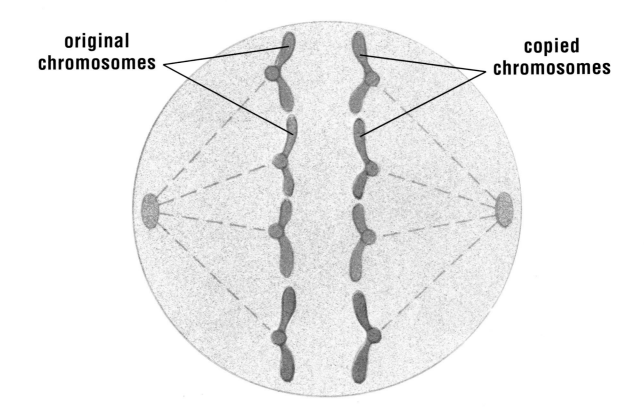

original
chromosomes

copied
chromosomes

When a nucleus gets ready to divide, the original
chromosomes and their copies line up in the middle
of the nucleus. Then they move to opposite sides of
the cell.

When a cell is ready to divide, it makes a copy of each
chromosome in its nucleus. The chromosomes separate
and move apart. Then the cell pinches in half and splits
into two separate cells. Each cell is exactly the same as
the original cell. Each has a full set of 46 chromosomes.

DID YOU KNOW?

Not all living things have the same number of chromosomes in their cells. Humans have 23 pairs of chromosomes, but cats have 19 pairs and wheat has 21 pairs. One kind of fern has approximately 630 pairs of chromosomes per cell! There is no link between how complex a living thing is and how many chromosomes it has.

BOY OR GIRL?

Sex cells—eggs and sperm—divide like other body cells at first. After copying the chromosomes, the cells split. Then these new cells split again. But this time, the chromosomes are not copied. The sperm and egg each end up with 23 single chromosomes.

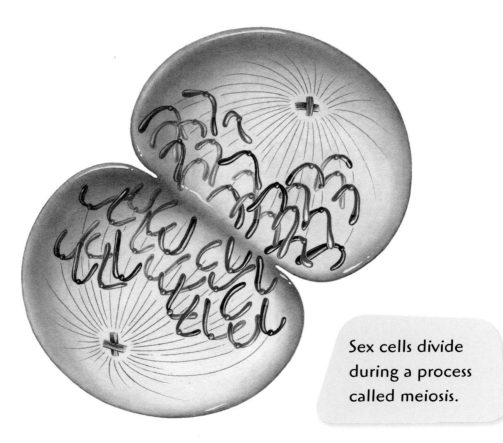

Sex cells divide during a process called meiosis.

If the egg and sperm come together, a living being is created. It will have 46 chromosomes—with half from the mother and half from the father. This mix of chromosomes allows for a huge number of combinations of genes. The new person's characteristics will come from his or her parents. But the person will have his or her own special genetic makeup.

DID YOU KNOW?

DNA can give you a glimpse into your family history. DNA testing can now show if two people are related and if they came from the same ancestor.

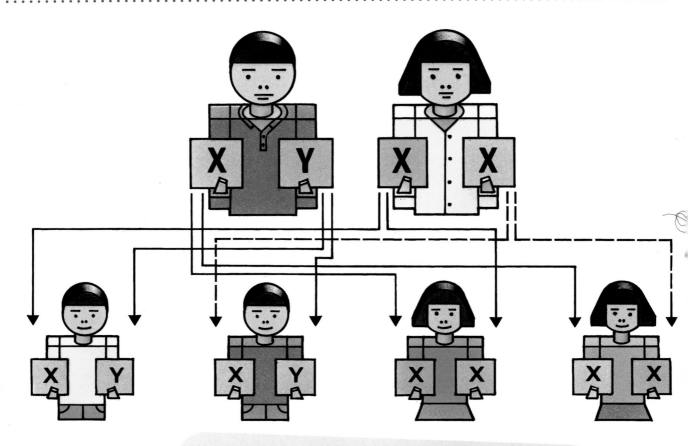

The father is the parent who determines a child's sex. If he passes along a Y, the child is male. If he passes along an X, the child is female.

Of the 23 pairs of chromosomes, one pair contains the genes that determine if a boy or girl will develop. These chromosomes are called X and Y. When a sperm and egg combine, two combinations are possible: XY and XX. An XY combination means a male will develop. An XX combination means a female will develop.

A mother can only pass along an X chromosome. But a father can pass along either an X or a Y chromosome. So, the father determines whether the offspring will be a boy or a girl.

Chapter 4

HOW TRAITS COMBINE

For centuries, farmers saved their best seeds from one year to plant and grow the next year's crops. People noticed that certain traits in the crops were passed along, but nobody understood how this happened.

Mendel studied science and math at the University of Vienna.

Gregor Mendel was a monk in an Austrian monastery. In the monastery's gardens and greenhouse in the 1800s, he carefully **bred** pea plants. He wanted to see what would happen when plants with different traits reproduced. Mendel studied seven traits, such as the colors of pea flowers and the shapes of seeds.

Mendel brushed pollen from the flower of one pea plant onto the flower of another plant. Pollen is a fine powder that plants use to reproduce. Then the flower from the second plant reproduced and made seeds. Mendel observed the new plants and recorded his findings. Then he bred the new plants.

Mendel crossed, or bred, purple-flowered plants with white-flowered plants. All of the resulting plants had purple flowers. But when Mendel crossed the new plants with one another, some plants had purple flowers and some had white flowers—all from parents with purple flowers!

In Mendel's studies, pea plants with white flowers appeared less often than pea plants with purple flowers.

Mendel found that the allele for purple flowers was dominant in pea plants.

Mendel continued the process over many generations of pea plants. From the results, he determined the basic laws of **heredity**. His laws apply to *all* life forms, not just pea plants.

Mendel's work showed that genes come in pairs. In each pair, one gene comes from the mother and

Scientists continue to use Mendel's findings to study genetics.

one comes from the father. So one gene pair may be responsible for a certain trait such as flower color.

However, each pair of genes can have two versions, or varieties, of the same trait. The gene for flower color can make white or purple petals. A different form of a gene is called an **allele**. The pea gene for flower color has an allele that makes white flowers and an allele that makes purple flowers.

Mendel also observed that often, one allele shows up in the plant but the other is hidden. He named the allele that shows up the **dominant** allele. When it was present, it masked the **recessive**, or hidden, allele. In other words, when purple and white pea flowers are crossed but all the new blooms are purple, then purple is the dominant trait and white is the recessive trait.

DID YOU KNOW?

Having brown eyes is a dominant trait, and having blue eyes is a recessive trait. This means that a brown-eyed mother and a blue-eyed father are likely to have a brown-eyed child. But the parents could have a blue-eyed child. For that to happen, the brown-eyed parent would have to pass along a recessive blue-eyed gene.

However, two blue-eyed parents can have only blue-eyed children. If both parents have blue eyes, this means that no brown-eyed allele is present among them. If it were present, the dominant gene would mask the blue-eyed one. The only genes the parents can pass on are for blue eyes.

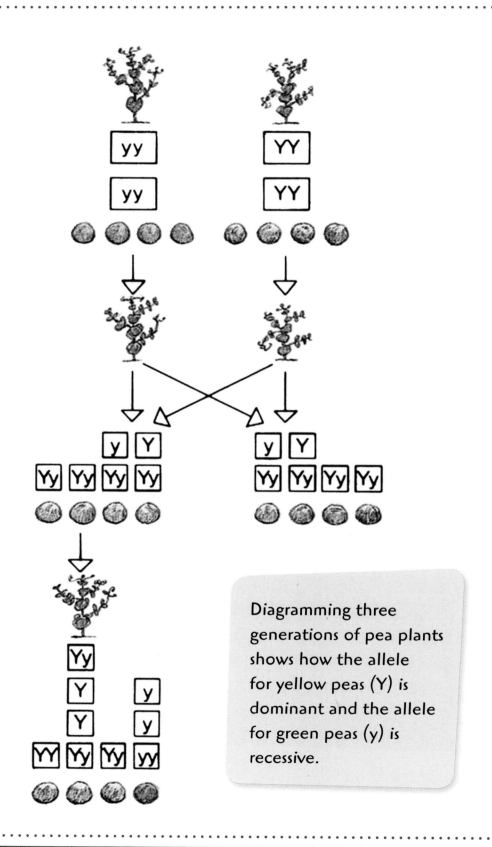

Diagramming three generations of pea plants shows how the allele for yellow peas (Y) is dominant and the allele for green peas (y) is recessive.

Mendel stated that the possible combinations of alleles are almost endless. Also, not all genes control single traits. Some traits are controlled by several genes, including height, eye color, and skin color. These genes can be on the same chromosome or on more than one chromosome.

DID YOU KNOW?

Genes in humans have alleles too. A kid may have an allele for freckles, while another family member might have the no-freckles allele. The same gene controls freckling. One allele says yes, and the other says no. Having freckles depends on which combination of alleles someone gets.

Chapter 5

PROBLEM GENES

Cell division allows for growth and replaces worn-out cells. It keeps the proper number of chromosomes in the sperm and egg cells. The division process also mixes up the genes to allow for variation, or differences, among offspring. But sometimes, things go wrong when cells divide.

Cells usually divide correctly, which keeps the body healthy.

Some changes in the DNA code do not affect the body's ability to function normally.

When a cell divides, the chromosomes are copied. Usually, the four bases of the DNA are copied in exactly the right order. But sometimes, one of the paired bases is copied with the wrong base. Sometimes, an extra base is included in the code. The changed gene reads the wrong code and makes an error when making a new cell.

Quite often, the tiny change does not have any effect. The body works with the change, so it does not make much difference. But sometimes, it does make a difference.

A gene **mutation** is a permanent change in the code of DNA. A mutation can be located on any single pair of any base step of the DNA ladder, or it may involve many steps. Inherited mutations occur when a changed gene is passed from parent to offspring. Acquired mutations are changes in DNA that develop during a person's lifetime.

A change in the DNA code can occur if the DNA bases pair up incorrectly. For example, thymine and guanine pairing together would cause a mutation.

DID YOU KNOW?

Every cell in the human body carries the same genetic information. Skin cells, eye cells, and heart cells all have the same genetic information. So, how do the cells know which of these things to make? Some genes control other genes and tell them to turn on and off. Information about the liver, for example, may be in skin cells. But the genes turn off the liver information in the skin and make certain that only the genes directing skin are working.

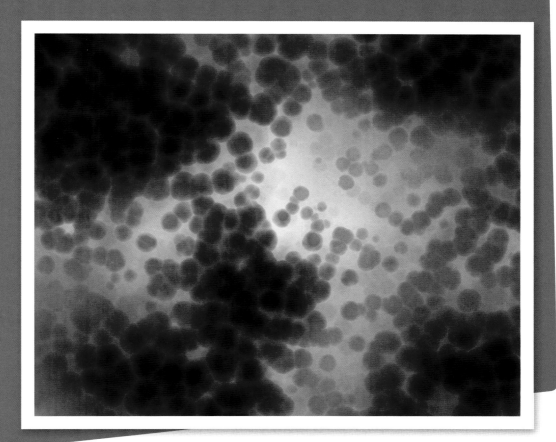

Many genetic diseases are recessive. A person may carry the allele for the disease but not actually have the disease because the normal gene is dominant. For the disease to show up, it must come from both parents.

Sickle cell anemia is one such disease. It occurs when a child gets two mutated genes—one from each parent. Anemia is a condition that results when the body does not have enough healthy red blood cells.

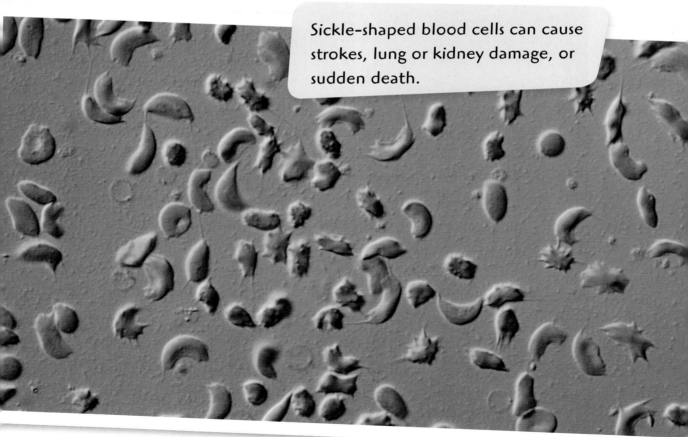

Sickle-shaped blood cells can cause strokes, lung or kidney damage, or sudden death.

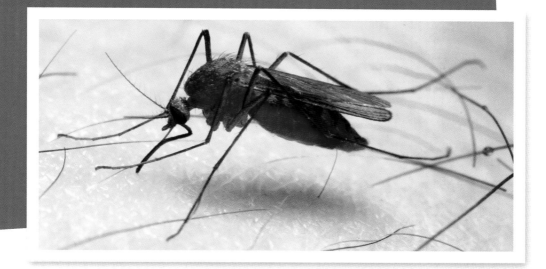

Normal red blood cells are shaped like disks with flattened centers. The curved sides of the blood cells let them slip through the blood vessels. In someone with sickle cell anemia, the red blood cells curve up on the sides. This prevents them from properly carrying oxygen, which is the job of normal blood cells. These curved cells do not live as long as normal red blood cells. Sometimes, the cells pile up and block the blood vessels because of their shape. This causes the person pain and damages his or her organs.

Other genetic conditions are also caused by chromosome problems. Each of the 46 chromosomes in humans contains thousands of genes. Someone who is born missing a chromosome usually will not survive. When a chromosome is missing, too much genetic information is left off for the cells to develop properly.

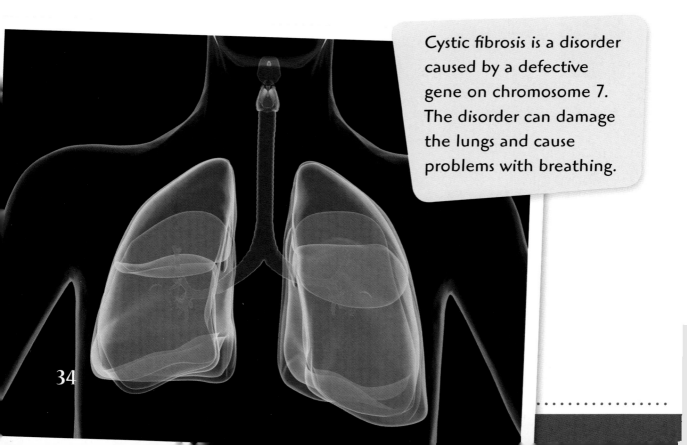

Cystic fibrosis is a disorder caused by a defective gene on chromosome 7. The disorder can damage the lungs and cause problems with breathing.

In some cases, a person may have a third chromosome in one of the pairs. Having an extra chromosome causes Down syndrome. This disorder delays a person's mental development and causes specific physical features, such as a flattened nose and upward-slanting eyes.

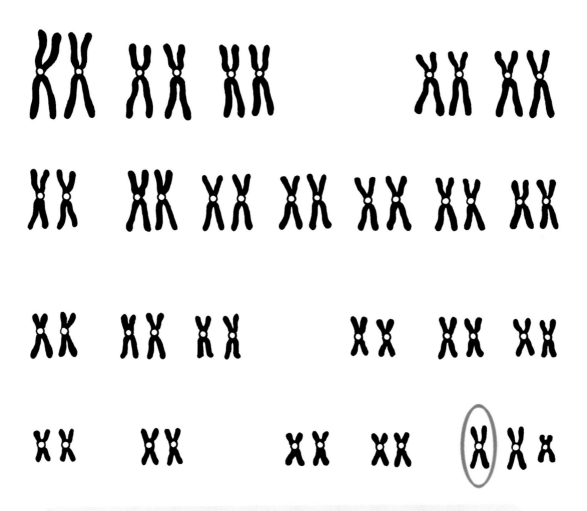

Most people have two copies of chromosome 21. People who have three copies develop Down syndrome.

Cancer is the uncontrollable growth of cells. Certain genes contain information to control cell growth and division. If these genes mutate, they cannot control cell growth. The cells grow out of control, and the cancer spreads.

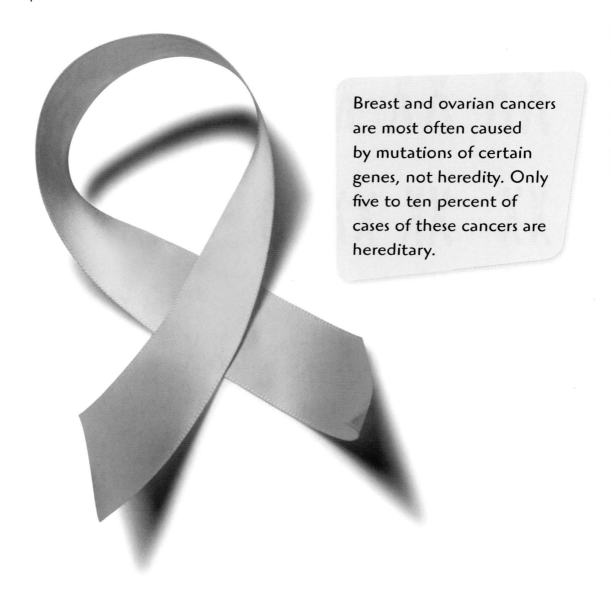

Breast and ovarian cancers are most often caused by mutations of certain genes, not heredity. Only five to ten percent of cases of these cancers are hereditary.

Scientists research to find treatments and cures for genetic disorders. Elizabeth Blackburn received a Nobel Prize in 2009 for her research on how chromosomes protect themselves during cell division.

More than one kind of mutation can cause cancer, which means cancer can develop in several ways. Some conditions in the environment appear to affect the development of cancer as well. For example, some chemicals in air, soil, and water have been linked to cancer. There is still much to be learned about cancer and the role genes play in causing it.

Chapter 6

THE FUTURE OF GENETICS

In 1990, the Human **Genome** Project brought together scientists from the United States, the United Kingdom, France, Germany, Japan, and China to identify the human genome. A genome is the complete set of DNA in a living **organism**. The scientists' goal was to identify the sequence of the genetic code in humans—all 3 billion base pairs on the 23 chromosomes. By 2003, the project had ended successfully.

Dr. Francis Collins, the director of the National Human Genome Research Institute, announced the success of the Human Genome Project in 2003.

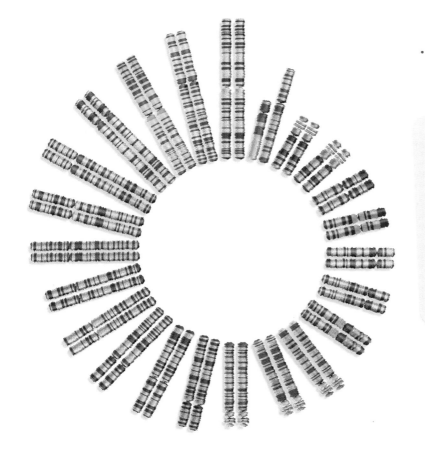

The model of the human genome shows the locations of specific genes on the 46 chromosomes.

The human genome acts as a blueprint for how the body works. The information gained about DNA from the Human Genome Project is being used for research in medicine, technology, and life science.

Genetic engineering is a method of removing, changing, or adding genes to DNA to change the information it carries. The altered DNA is inserted inside bacteria and viruses. Bacteria and virus cells are useful because they replicate in the body. When the bacteria and viruses are put inside a living thing, they reproduce cells that have the changed DNA.

Genetic engineering has been used on food. Crops have been changed to resist pests and diseases and to improve the quantity and quality of foods they produce. Golden rice is an example of a genetically modified food. It contains the nutrient beta-carotene, which is changed to vitamin A in the body.

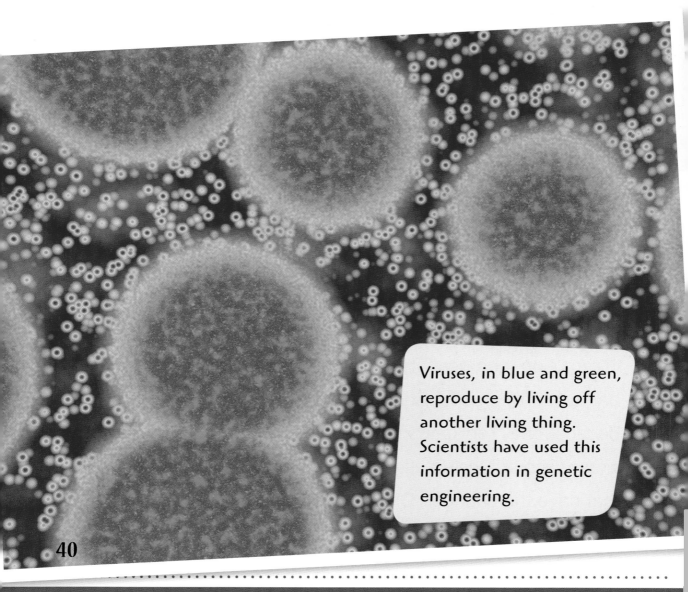

Viruses, in blue and green, reproduce by living off another living thing. Scientists have used this information in genetic engineering.

Soybeans are one kind of crop that has been genetically modified.

Cloning is a method of taking DNA from one living thing and inserting it into an egg cell, where it grows into an exact copy of the original organism. The DNA of the two organisms is identical. Cloning made the news in 1997 when Dolly the sheep became the first animal to be cloned. It took scientists almost 300 attempts to get it right, though.

Cloning might be used in the future to produce animals for use in studying diseases and treatments. Also, endangered animals that are not breeding might be reproduced and put back into the wild. Organs might be cloned as "spare parts" to replace defective ones in humans. However, a lot of research is still needed for cloning to become a part of everyday science and medicine.

How Dolly Was Cloned

A donor cell is taken from a sheep's udder.

Donor Nucleus

The two cells are fused using an electric shock.

Fused Cell

Egg Cell

The nucleus of the egg cell is removed.

The fused cell begins dividing normally.

An egg cell is taken from an adult female sheep.

Embryo

The embryo is placed in the uterus of a foster mother.

The embryo develops normally into a lamb—Dolly.

Cloned Lamb

Foster Mother

Dolly died at age six in 2003.

Some scientists who research and experiment with cloning study how to transfer cells from one living thing to another.

Genetic engineering and cloning seem to hold the answers to genetic problems. But these scientific methods also raise many concerns. They are often expensive and unreliable, and many people worry about harmful effects they could have. Scientists will continue to explore genetics and genetic engineering in many more years of research.

DID YOU KNOW?

Each person has his or her own **DNA fingerprint**. In other words, a person's **DNA** code is unique. Detectives often search crime scenes for evidence that carries **DNA**, such as hair and blood. In a laboratory, the **DNA** evidence can be checked against the **DNA** of known criminals. If a match is made, this might help detectives solve the crime.

Glossary

allele (uh-LEEL): one of two alternate forms of a gene that allows for different traits

bred (BRED): to have made living things reproduce under a controlled environment

chromosomes (KROH-muh-sohms): the tight coil of information in the nucleus of a cell that contains an organism's genetic code

deoxyribonucleic acid (dee-OK-see-rye-boh-noo-klee-uhk AS-id): DNA; the coded genetic material that makes up each individual

dominant (DOM-uh-nuhnt): a trait that appears in an offspring if one of the parents contributes it

gene (JEEN): a tiny unit that carries the code for inherited traits in chromosomes

genetic engineering (juh-NET-ik en-juh-NIHR-ing): a method of removing, changing, or adding genes to DNA to change the information it carries

genetics (juh-NET-iks): the branch of science that studies heredity

genome (JEE-nohm): the complete set of DNA in an organism

heredity (huh-RED-uh-tee): the passing of genes from parent to offspring

mutation (myoo-TAY-shuhn): a change in the code of DNA

offspring (OFF-spring): the young produced by parents, such as the children of humans and the seeds that grow new plants

organism (OR-guh-niz-uhm): a living thing

recessive (ree-SESS-ihv): a trait that must be contributed by both parents in order to show in an offspring

species (SPEE-sheez): a group of living things that share similar traits and can reproduce with each other

Index

Websites to Visit

learn.genetics.utah.edu/content/begin/dna/

library.thinkquest.org/28599/

www.brainpop.com/science/cellularlifeandgenetics/

www.neok12.com/Genetics.htm

About the Author

Shirley Duke writes fiction and nonfiction for children. She has always loved science. She taught science, reading, and English as a second language in the public schools for 25 years at the elementary, middle, and high school levels. She holds a bachelor's degree in biology and a master's degree in education from Austin College. Her hobbies include reading, gardening, and cooking. She grew up in Dallas and lives with her husband in Garland, Texas.